Social Studies Explorer

IRAN

◆ by G. S. Prentzas

CHERRY LAKE PUBLISHING • ANN ARBOR, MICHIGAN

Published in the United States of America
by Cherry Lake Publishing
Ann Arbor, Michigan
www.cherrylakepublishing.com

Book design and production: The Design Lab

Cover, ©Vladimir Melnik/Dreamstime.com; cover (stamp), ©Hank Frentz/Dreamstime.com;
page 4, ©zerega/Alamy; pages 5 and 28, ©MARKA/Alamy; page 6, ©steba/Shutterstock,
Inc.; page 8, ©INTERFOTO/Alamy; pages 9, 14, 23, 26, 32, and 36, ©ASSOCIATED PRESS;
pages 10, ©EmmePi Travel/Alamy; page 13, ©imagebroker/Alamy; page 15, ©North Wind
Picture Archives/Alamy; page 16, ©Panos Karapanagiotis/Shutterstock, Inc.; page 17,
©Robert Harding Picture Library Ltd/Alamy; page 18, ©Everett Collection Inc/Alamy; page
20, ©pdesign/Shutterstock, Inc.; page 21, ©Glyn Thomas/Alamy; page 22, ©epa european
pressphoto agency b.v./Alamy; page 24, ©dbimages/Alamy; page 34, ©roger parkes/Alamy;
page 40, ©Andrea Skjold/Shutterstock, Inc.; page 42, ©Karen Grigoryan/Shutterstock, Inc.;
page 45, ©Kamyar Adl/Alamy

Library of Congress Cataloging-in-Publication Data
Prentzas, G. S.
  Iran/by G.S. Prentzas.
      p. cm.—(Social studies explorer) (It's cool to learn about countries)
  Includes bibliographical references and index.
  ISBN 978-1-61080-440-0 (lib. bdg.) — ISBN 978-1-61080-527-8 (e-book) —
ISBN 978-1-61080-614-5 (pbk.)
  1. Iran—Juvenile literature. I. Title.
  DS254.75.P74 2012
  955—dc23   2012001714

Cherry Lake Publishing would like to acknowledge the work of The Partnership for
21st Century Skills. Please visit www.21stcenturyskills.org for more information.

Printed in the United States of America
Corporate Graphics Inc.
July 2012
CLFA11

TABLE OF CONTENTS

CHAPTER ONE

WELCOME TO IRAN!

➥ Snowy mountain peaks are a common part of Iran's geography.

Would you like to explore Iran? Get ready to discover a country rich in history and culture. Iran's story goes back thousands of years. The Persians, one of several groups of people who lived in ancient Iran, built a powerful empire in southwestern Asia. Today, almost 78 million people call Iran home.

What type of land comes to mind when you think of Iran? If you imagine rugged, snowcapped mountain ranges, you are right! But Iran offers much more than mountains. It is also home to remote deserts and fertile lowlands that border ocean gulfs and saltwater lakes.

Iran stretches across 636,374 square miles (1,648,200 square kilometers) of southwestern Asia. That makes it a little larger than the state of Alaska. The Caspian Sea and the countries of Armenia, Azerbaijan, and Turkmenistan sit along Iran's northern

The beaches along the Caspian Sea are popular spots for Iranians to relax.

border. Afghanistan and Pakistan lie to its east. The waves of the Gulf of Oman break along Iran's southern shores. Along its southwestern coast, the waters of the Persian Gulf separate Iran from the Arabian Peninsula. Iraq and Turkey border Iran to the west.

Iran's capital and biggest city is Tehran. Around 12 million people live in Tehran and its **suburbs**. The city lies at the foot of the Alborz Mountains in northern Iran. It sits about 66 miles (106 km) from the Caspian Sea. The Caspian Sea is the world's largest **landlocked** body of water. It is about 750 miles (1,207 km) long and 250 miles (402 km) wide. Most scientists consider

➡ Tehran is a huge city with many suburbs.

ASIA

EUROPE

IRAN

Atlantic Ocean

Arctic Ocean

Mediterranean Sea

Indian Ocean

AFRICA

Atlantic Ocean

IRAN

•➤ Iran is located in the southwestern part of Asia.

the Caspian Sea to be the world's largest lake. But many people call it a sea because it has salty water.

Much of Iran's terrain is rugged. The country has several large mountain ranges. The Alborz Mountains are located in the north, between Tehran and the Caspian Sea. Iran's highest peak, Mount Damavand, lies

⟶ The Dasht-e Lut is a very dry, salty desert.

in the Alborz range. It has an elevation of 18,605 feet
(5,671 meters) and is covered with snow all year. The
Zagros Mountains stretch across western Iran.

Iran's mountain ranges surround remote deserts and
dry plains. Iran has two large deserts. The smaller one is
called the Dasht-e Lut and is located in eastern Iran. The
larger one, called the Dasht-e Kavir, is unusual. A crusty
layer of salt covers it. This coating forms when salty
water runs down from the mountains after rainfalls and
creates puddles on the desert's dry floor. When the water
in these pools **evaporates**, salt crystals are left behind.

Iran also has two small lowland regions. One sits along the coast of the Caspian Sea. This area has fertile soil and produces much of the nation's agricultural products. The oil-rich Khuzestan Plain lies north of the Persian Gulf.

Most Iranians live near the foothills of the mountains because those areas have the most water. Rain and melted snow from the mountains create small streams and lakes in these regions. In addition to Tehran, major cities in Iran include Mashhad (2.41 million), Esfahan (1.60 million), Tabriz (1.39 million), Karaj (1.37 million), and Shiraz (1.2 million).

Iran is located where three sections of the earth's crust meet. As a result, many strong earthquakes have occurred throughout the country's history. In 2003, a powerful earthquake struck the desert city of Bam, killing more than 25,000 people. Although Bam's residents have rebuilt much of their city, the earthquake has had a lasting effect on families who lost homes or loved ones in the disaster.

Iran has only a few major rivers. The Karun River flows more than 500 miles (800 km) through the western part of the country. It is the only river in Iran that ships can use, making it an important transportation route. It allows Iran to send its valuable oil to world markets. The Zayandeh River is located in central Iran. The Safid River is the longest in the country. It lies in northwestern Iran and flows into the Caspian Sea. Lake Urmia is Iran's largest lake and is also located in northwestern Iran. Its salty waters cover about 2,000 square miles (5,180 sq km).

➨ Si-o-Seh Pol is one of many elaborate bridges that cross over the Zayandeh River.

Take a close look at this map of Iran. Then place a separate piece of paper over it. Carefully trace the outline of the country. Draw a star to mark Tehran's location. Then add Iran's other major cities to your map. Draw the Karun and Safid Rivers, as well as Lake Urmia. Use an atlas or online map to mark the locations of Iran's two main deserts. Label the other land features that you have just read about. Think about where the country's cities are located. What do most of them have in common?

If you're visiting Iran, what clothes should you pack? In most places, you'll need a jacket or sweater. Iran's mountains and highlands are usually cool or freezing. Even the deserts get chilly at night. The country's climate varies from region to region. Temperatures differ greatly from one season to the next. They also vary between the northern and southern parts of the country. In winter, the temperatures in most of the country are cold. Heavy snowfalls are common in the mountains. But along the Persian Gulf and the Gulf of Oman, winters are warm. These lowland areas also have hot, humid summers. Temperatures often top 100 degrees Fahrenheit (37.8 degrees Celsius). Temperatures soar even higher in Iran's deserts. They can reach as high as 120°F (48.9°C)!

Much of Iran is dry. The northern and western parts of the country get most of the rainfall. The farming region along the Caspian Sea gets about 80 inches (203 centimeters) of rain each year. The eastern and southeastern parts of Iran are much drier. Some areas in southeastern Iran get less than 2 inches (5 cm) of rain annually. That is about the same as California's Death Valley! The valleys between Iran's mountain ridges get about 40 inches (102 cm) of rain each year. The availability of water makes these areas good places for people to live and grow crops.

Iran's forests are home to a wide variety of plant species.

In dry regions, prickly shrubs, short grasses, palm trees, and other plants have adapted to the lack of water. The rainy areas along the shores of the Caspian Sea have forests full of oaks, elms, and other trees. Wildflowers grow in areas that have enough water.

Many types of wildlife live in Iran's forests, including leopards, sheep, and boars. Snakes, lizards, and other

Asiatic cheetahs once lived throughout much of Asia. They ranged from the Arabian Peninsula to eastern India. Today, they are extinct in all Asian countries except Iran. Wildlife conservation officials estimate that only about 120 of these large cats still live in the wild. They are found in remote areas around the Dasht-e Kavir desert. Asiatic cheetahs, along with their African relatives, are the world's fastest land animals. They can reach top speeds of about 70 miles per hour (113 kph)!

animals live in Iran's drier regions. About 500 species of birds live in Iran. Some live in Iran all year, but others stay there only during certain seasons. Shrimp and catfish are among the aquatic animals that live in the Caspian Sea, the Persian Gulf, the Gulf of Oman, and Iran's rivers and lakes.

BUSINESS AND GOVERNMENT

➥ Cyrus the Great expanded Persia's range significantly during his years as its ruler.

The history of modern Iran's government goes back more than 5,000 years. A group of people known as the Elamites settled northeast of the Persian Gulf around 3000 BCE. They created Iran's first kingdom. About 1,500 years later, people called the Aryans settled in what is now southwestern Iran. Their descendants split into two major groups. The Persians lived in southern Iran. The Medes settled in northern and western Iran.

Cyrus the Great ruled Persia from 580 to 529 BCE. When his army defeated the Medes, he combined the two kingdoms to create the first Persian Empire. Darius I became the empire's king in 522 BCE. His armies conquered other nearby regions, expanding the Persian Empire to its greatest size. At the time, it was the world's largest empire. Under Darius I, the Persian Empire stretched north almost to the area that is present-day Russia, east to India, and west to Egypt. The first Persian Empire ended in 330 BCE, when Macedonia's Alexander the Great invaded Persia and defeated its army.

➥ A statue of Alexander the Great stands in Greece, at the former site of Macedonia's capital.

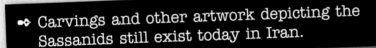

➡ Carvings and other artwork depicting the Sassanids still exist today in Iran.

Beginning in the third century BCE, Persia was ruled by a group of people called the Parthians. The Second Persian Empire arose when the Sassanid **dynasty** seized control from the Parthians in 224 CE. The Sassanid kings restored many Persian traditions and customs that had disappeared under Macedonian rule. In the 630s, an Arab army began invading Persia. The Arabs introduced their religion, Islam, to the Persians.

The Safavi Empire arose in the sixteenth century when 15-year-old Ismail Safavi took control of the

⇥ Mohammad Ali Shah led Persia for less than three years before he was overthrown.

country. Under the rule of Ismail and his descendants, Persians adopted Shia Islam, one of the religion's major **denominations**. The Qajar dynasty gained control of Persia in 1796. Its kings ruled the country until 1925.

Persia adopted its first constitution in 1906. The new king, Mohammad Ali Shah, tried to suspend the constitution two years later. A revolt forced him to leave the country. In 1924, Persian military officer Reza Khan became the head of the government. The next year, he took the title of shah. Reza Shah's government built public schools and railroads in an effort to modernize the country.

However, his rule also oppressed the country's people, and **corruption** was a major problem in the government. Reza Shah soon became unpopular with many of Persia's people.

In 1935, the government of Reza Shah began asking foreign countries to call the country Iran instead of Persia. The country is now known around the world as Iran, and its people are called Iranians. The word *Iran* means "of the Aryans."

During World War II, Soviet and British armies occupied Iran. They forced the shah to hand his throne to his son, Mohammad Reza. Mohammad Reza tried to fulfill his father's dream of a modern Iran by building schools, hospitals, and roads. However, he was a harsh dictator. Many of Iran's religious leaders believed that the new shah was too forceful a ruler. They spoke out against him, and the Iranian public soon began turning against the shah. In response, Mohammad Reza outlawed all political parties except his own. Police jailed Iranians who disagreed with the shah.

The opposition to the shah grew into a full-fledged revolution. The shah fled Iran in 1979. A religious leader, **Ayatollah** Ruhollah Khomeini, took charge of Iran's government. That same year, the U.S. government allowed the former shah to enter the United States for medical treatment. In protest, Iranian students stormed the U.S. **embassy** in Tehran. They took 66 Americans

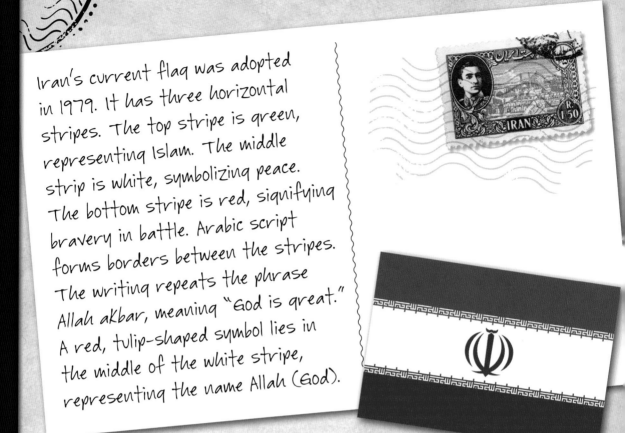

Iran's current flag was adopted in 1979. It has three horizontal stripes. The top stripe is green, representing Islam. The middle strip is white, symbolizing peace. The bottom stripe is red, signifying bravery in battle. Arabic script forms borders between the stripes. The writing repeats the phrase Allah akbar, meaning "God is great." A red, tulip-shaped symbol lies in the middle of the white stripe, representing the name Allah (God).

hostage. The students held the hostages for more than a year. The incident soured the relationship between Iran and the United States.

In 1980, the neighboring country of Iraq invaded Iran and attempted to take control of the oil-rich Khuzestan plain. The two countries fought a long, bloody war that lasted for most of the decade. Hundreds of thousands of people died on both sides, including many civilians. Fighting did not end until 1988, and peace was not made official until 1990.

The rial is Iran's standard currency. Rials are available in coins and paper money. In May 2012, one U.S. dollar equaled 12,500 rials.

Iranians often use the term toman to indicate 10 rials. The toman was an earlier type of currency used in Iran.

When Khomeini died in 1989, Sayyid Ali Khamenei took over as Iran's supreme leader. In 1997, Mohammad Khatami won the presidential election. During his eight years in office, he tried to restore relations with the United States and other countries. However, conservative religious leaders held the real power, and they prevented Khatami's reforms. In 2005, Mahmoud Ahmadinejad won the presidency. At first, he guided the country in the direction desired by Iran's religious leaders. In recent years, however, Ahmadinejad and the religious leaders have been at odds.

In the 2000s, Iran's nuclear program brought it into conflict with the United States, Israel, and other countries. World leaders worried that Iran was trying to build nuclear weapons, but Iran's government insisted that it was only developing nuclear energy technology.

Iran adopted a new constitution after the 1979 revolution. The government outlined in this constitution continues to rule the country today. The supreme leader is the head of the government. Iran's Assembly of Experts, a group of 83 religious leaders, appoints the supreme leader, who serves for life. He has the power to reject any decisions by the president or the legislature.

➻ The Assembly of Experts holds a great deal of power in the Iranian government.

➥ Mahmoud Ahmadinejad was elected president of Iran in 2005.

He also appoints military officers, judges, and the members of the Expediency Council, which has the power to supervise all of the branches of Iran's government.

Iran's government is divided into executive, legislative, and judicial branches. The president heads the executive branch. He is elected to a four-year term and oversees the operation of the government.

Iran's legislature is called the Majlis. It has 290 members who are elected to four-year terms. They write the nation's laws and approve the government's budget. The 12 members of the Guardian Council make sure that all laws observe Islamic principles.

Iran's judicial branch has one Supreme Court that hears appeals. Many lower courts handle criminal cases and civil lawsuits. In Iran, Islamic law determines all legal matters. For example, Iranians cannot drink alcohol. Women must wear headscarves and cover their arms and legs in public. The country has a special court called the Islamic Revolutionary Court. It hears cases involving serious violations of Islamic law. These crimes include **blasphemy** and attempts to overthrow the government.

How do Iranians make a living? About 45 percent of the nation's workers have service jobs. People with service jobs do not make goods or produce farm products.

ACTIVITY

IRAN

In 2010, Iran produced about $357 billion worth of goods and services. Agricultural goods made up almost 11 percent of this amount. Services represented nearly 48 percent. About 41 percent of the nation's total economic value was connected to industrial products. Use this information to create a bar graph to show how different areas of the Iranian economy contributed to the total value of the country's goods and services in 2010.

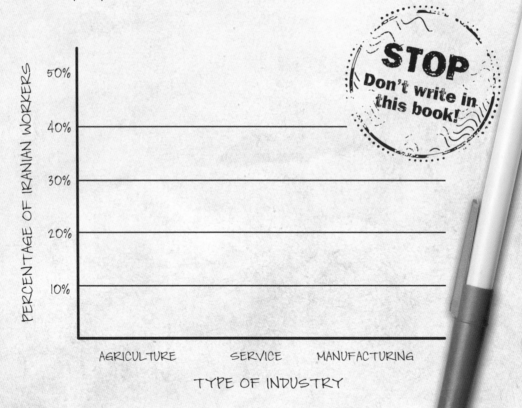

STOP
Don't write in this book!

PERCENTAGE OF IRANIAN WORKERS

50%

40%

30%

20%

10%

AGRICULTURE   SERVICE   MANUFACTURING

TYPE OF INDUSTRY

They perform services for other people. Service workers include store clerks, police officers, and teachers.

About 31 percent of Iranian workers have jobs in industry. Most of Iran's industrial products are based on the country's natural resources. Iran's largest industries are oil and natural gas production. Iran has the world's third-largest oil reserves and second-largest natural gas reserves. Other important industries include coal, copper, iron ore, and zinc. Around 25 percent of Iran's laborers

➥ Oil plays a major role in the Iranian economy.

have agricultural jobs. Farmers grow wheat, rice, and other grains. They also grow sugar beets, sugarcane, fruits, and nuts. They produce dairy products, cotton, and wool.

IMPORT EXPORT

Do you want to understand Iran's economy better? Look at the things it imports and exports. Imports are goods and services that a country buys from other countries. Exports are goods and services that a country sells to other countries. Here are some of Iran's top imports and exports:

IMPORTS ⟶ IRAN ⟶ EXPORTS

IMPORTS	EXPORTS
industrial supplies	petroleum
capital goods	chemical products
food	petrochemical products
consumer goods	fruits and nuts
technical services	carpets

CHAPTER THREE

MEET THE PEOPLE

➠ Many Iranian people live traditional lives in rural villages.

Nearly 78 million people live in Iran. Most Iranians live in large cities such as Tehran. Only about one-fourth of the country's people live in small villages and rural areas.

About 98 percent of Iran's people are Muslim, which means they follow the religion of Islam. Islam is based on the life and teachings of the Prophet Muhammad. Most Iranian Muslims follow the Shia denomination. They believe that Islamic religious leaders must be directly descended from Ali, a follower and cousin of Muhammad. About 10 percent of Iranians are Sunni Muslims. However, more than three-quarters of the world's 1.6 billion Muslims are Sunni. Most Shias live in Iran and Iraq, though there are also many in Pakistan, Lebanon, and other nations. Other Iranians practice a range of religions, including Zoroastrianism, Judaism, Christianity, and Baha'i.

Iran is home to many different **ethnic** groups. Persians make up about 61 percent of the population. The country's main ethnic minority groups are the Azeris and the Kurds. Most Azeris and Kurds in Iran live in the northwestern region of the country. A group of people known as Lurs lives in western Iran, near the border with Iraq. Small populations of Balochs, Arabs, Turkmens, and many other ethnic groups also live in Iran.

Iran's official language is Persian, but some Iranians speak other languages. Kurds speak Kurdish, which is closely related to Persian. Various ethnic minorities have their own languages. For example, Lurs speak Lur, Balochs speak Balochi, and Arabs speak Arabic.

The Persian language is written in Arabic script. However, Persian is not related to the Arabic language. It is related to English, Spanish, Hindi, and other languages. Many Persian words have made their way into English. Have you ever used the words bazaar, jackal, jungle, kebab, lemon, orange, pistachio, or rose? They all come from the Persian language!

Iranian children are required to attend school between the ages of 6 and 11. After that, education is optional. The government provides free public education, including college, to all students. Some wealthy families pay to send their children to private schools and colleges.

Parents can send children younger than 6 years old to preschool. From primary school through secondary school, boys and girl are taught in separate classes. Primary school consists of grades one through five. Grades six through eight make up what is known as the middle cycle. Students in grades nine to twelve attend secondary schools. There are two different types of

secondary schools. In academic schools, students study literature, math, science, and other subjects. In work-training schools, students prepare for jobs in business, industry, or agriculture. Students choose which type of school they want to attend.

Because more than half of Iran's population is 25 years old or younger, education is an important issue for Iranians. The country has more than 113,000 schools. About 1 million teachers instruct more than 18 million students. Nearly 95 percent of Iran's students now receive primary and secondary education.

Students must pass a national exam to move from primary school to the middle cycle or from the middle cycle to secondary school. Secondary school graduates must score highly on another national exam to attend college. This exam is very competitive. Iran's colleges have a limited number of spots for new students each year.

CHAPTER FOUR

CELEBRATIONS!

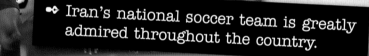

➥ Iran's national soccer team is greatly admired throughout the country.

What do Iran's people do for fun? Like many people around the world, they play or watch sports, spend time with friends and family, and celebrate religious and national holidays.

Wrestling and soccer are the two biggest sports in Iran. Weight lifting, bodybuilding, polo, tae kwon do, and skiing are also very popular.

Freestyle wrestling is considered Iran's national sport.

This love of wrestling grew out of the fondness Iranians have for *koshti*, the traditional Persian style of wrestling. Like other types of wrestling, koshti requires quickness, good technique, and physical endurance. Iranian wrestlers have achieved great international success. They have won more than 30 Olympic medals in wrestling.

Soccer, or football, has become Iran's most popular sport to play and to watch. Iran has several professional soccer leagues. Professional soccer games draw thousands of fans. The 18-team Iran Pro League is the country's top league. Esteghlal, Persepolis, and Sepahan have been the league's most successful clubs. Iran's national soccer team is called Team Melli, meaning "national team." Team Melli has won three Asian Cup finals and played in three World Cup competitions. Some of Iran's biggest soccer stars include center forward Ali Daei and midfielder Karim Bagheri. Both are now retired players.

Family is central to Iranian life. Iranian families spend a lot of time together at home. People also meet friends for tea at cafés and get together before and after praying at **mosques**. Iranian law forbids men and women to socialize in public if they are not married or otherwise related to each other. Public places, such as theaters and pools, have separate sections for men and women. Although their interaction with men is limited, women in Iran take an active role in society. They attend school, work, and vote.

A sofreh includes such objects as seeds, apples, garlic, vinegar, a gold coin, and a goldfish.

People in Iran celebrate many holidays with family members and friends. The country's biggest holiday starts on the first day of spring. Noruz, or Persian New Year, is a 13-day celebration that begins on March 21. The holiday honors the new life that spring brings. To prepare for the holiday, Iranians clean their homes thoroughly. They also visit family members and give presents to children.

For the formal celebration of Noruz, a family sets up a *sofreh*. A sofreh is a special table or a large tablecloth spread on the floor of the main room in the home. Iranians put several items on the sofreh and leave them there during the entire holiday. An open holy book, such as the Koran for Muslim families, is one of the items. Candles are also set on the sofreh. They are lit to represent the warmth of spring. Other items on the sofreh symbolize certain ideals. For example, an apple stands for good health.

Iran also has several other national holidays. Many of these holidays celebrate the 1979 revolution that overthrew the shah. These holidays are Victory of the Islamic Revolution (February 11), Islamic Republic Day (April 1), and Day of the **Martyrs** of the Revolution (September 8). On June 3, a national holiday remembers the death of Ayatollah Khomeini.

Each year, Iranian families grow wheatgrass from seeds as part of the Noruz celebration. The wheatgrass sprouts, called sabzeh, represent the renewal of nature during spring. The 13th and final day of Noruz is known as sizdah bedar. Iranians leave their home and spend the day in the countryside. Many Iranians throw the wheatgrass shoots they've grown into a river or other body of water. This ceremony symbolizes a person getting rid of the previous year's problems and hoping for good luck in the new year.

People in Iran also celebrate religious holidays. The Muslim holiday of Ramadan begins in the ninth month of the Islamic calendar. For the entire month, Muslims do not eat or drink from sunrise to sunset. They believe that this **fast** purifies the body and improves a person's commitment to the teachings of Islam. Muslims observe the end of Ramadan with a three-day celebration called Eid al-Fitr. People visit their extended families and exchange gifts. Many families prepare a special meal to celebrate.

Iranians celebrate Eid al-Fitr in a variety of ways.

MAKE A KITE

Flying kites is a popular pastime for kids and adults in Iran. A yearly kite festival in Tehran allows kite builders to show off many different types of kites. You can make your own kite with some simple materials.

MATERIALS
- Masking tape
- One 36-inch (91 cm) piece of flat wood or a round wooden dowel, 0.25-inch (0.64 cm) wide
- One 33-inch (84 cm) piece of flat wood or a round wooden dowel, 0.25-inch (0.64 cm) wide
- A small saw or knife
- Tape measure
- Pencil
- A ball of strong string
- Scissors
- One large plastic bag
- At least six 12-inch (30 cm) strips of cloth, about 2 inches (5 cm) wide

INSTRUCTIONS

1. Wrap a layer of masking tape around the ends of both pieces of wood. With an adult helping, use the saw or knife to make a notch in the center of both ends of both wood pieces. You will use the notches later.

2. Lay the 36-inch (91 cm) piece vertically, meaning up and down, on your work surface. Use the tape measure to measure 10 inches (25 cm) down from the top of the wood. Draw a line on the wood with the pencil.

3. Place the 33-inch (84 cm) piece of wood on top of the 36-inch (91 cm) piece horizontally, or side to side. Use string to tie the two pieces of wood together. Tie the string tightly so that the two pieces of wood won't come apart. Wrap masking tape over the string to secure it.

4. Starting at the bottom of the frame, wrap the string around the wooden frame. Make sure the string sits in the notch on each end of the frame.

5. Tape over each end of the frame to make sure the string does not pop out of the notches.

6. Tighten the string and tie it off at the bottom of the frame. Use the scissors to cut the string off the ball.

7. Cut the sides of the plastic bag to make a large sheet of plastic. Lay it flat on your work surface.

8. Lay the frame on the piece of plastic. Use the scissors to cut the plastic so that it's about an inch (2.54 cm) larger than the frame on all four sides.

9. Fold the plastic ends on one side over the frame. Tape along the entire edge to join the plastic ends to the main sheet of plastic. Repeat on the other three sides of the frame.

10. Cut a 6-foot (1.8 m) piece of string and tie it to the bottom of the kite. Measure down the string 1 foot (0.3 m) from the frame. At this spot, tie one of the strips of cloth to the string. Tie five more strips of cloth to the string so that they are about 1 foot (0.3 m) apart.

11. Attach the finished kite to a long ball of string. Take extra string and strips of cloth so that you can add more cloth strips if your kite isn't flying straight.

CHAPTER FIVE

WHAT'S FOR DINNER?

→ Chelo kebab is a healthy and delicious dish.

Do you like rice? Farmers have grown rice in Iran for more than 3,000 years. It is the main ingredient in many of the country's most popular dishes. Iran's national dish is *chelo* kebab, which is rice topped with grilled meat.

Making chelo is not as simple as simmering rice in water. It takes a lot of time. Cooks rinse the rice grains several times before boiling them in salted water. The rice is then drained and steamed in a pan of water, along with butter, saffron, and sometimes yogurt. This

cooking method produces fluffy rice grains that don't stick together. If you're a guest in an Iranian home where chelo is being served, your host may offer you the crusty layer of chelo rice that sticks to the bottom of the pan. It is considered a special treat.

Chelo isn't the only Iranian dish made from rice. Cooks make a basic rice dish called *katteh* by simmering rice grains in water. *Shireen polo* is a much fancier dish. It is made by mixing cooked rice with shredded carrot, orange peel, almonds, pistachios, dried fruit, saffron, and meat.

In addition to rice, Iranian meals often contain wheat, lamb, poultry, yogurt, and eggplant. Spinach, beans, and rose water are other common ingredients.

Cooks in Iran use the spice saffron in many traditional dishes. Thin strands of saffron are found inside a certain type of crocus flower. Saffron threads must be picked by hand. It takes 75,000 flowers to make 1 pound (0.45 kilograms) of saffron! Because it takes so much work to harvest, saffron is the world's most expensive spice. It tastes spicy and slightly bitter. It also makes food turn an orange-red color.

➥ Sangak is one of the many tasty breads eaten in Iran.

Cooks in Iran use many different herbs and spices. They also use lots of butter and oil.

Popular dishes in Iran include vegetables stuffed with grains, grilled and stewed meats, and fruit sauces. Cooks also make thick vegetable soups, flavoring them with lemon, lime, or sour orange juice. *Barbari* is a thick, crusty bread usually eaten for breakfast. *Sangak* is a thin bread often used to make sandwiches.

In addition to lamb and chicken, fish is popular in Iran. Anglers catch herring, sturgeon, and other cold-water fish in the Caspian Sea. They catch tuna, swordfish, and other warm-water fish in the Persian Gulf and the Sea of Oman. People who live near the coast often eat fresh fish. Most Iranians in the interior regions rarely have fresh fish. They use dried, salted fish in their dishes.

Would you like to enjoy a flavorful Iranian dish that you can make yourself? Mast-o-Khiyar is a soup made with cucumber, yogurt, and mint. Thicker versions of mast-o-khiyar are eaten as a dip. Iranian cooks add various fruits and nuts to the basic ingredients to create a refreshing dish for a hot summer day.

Mast-o-Khiyar

INGREDIENTS
2 cucumbers
Salt
1 ounce (28 grams) currants
1 ounce (28 g) walnuts
15 mint leaves
32 ounces (907 g) Greek yogurt
Fresh or dried dill (optional)

GREEK YOGURT

INSTRUCTIONS

1. Peel the cucumbers and chop them into tiny pieces. Place the chopped cucumber bits in a bowl. Sprinkle them with salt and let them sit for at least 30 minutes.

2. Soak the currants in a bowl of water for about 15 minutes. Drain the water.

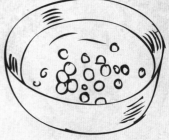

3. Chop the walnuts into small pieces.

4. Wash the mint leaves. Dry the leaves and chop them into small pieces.

5. Squeeze the excess water out of the chopped cucumbers and place them in a large bowl. Add the yogurt, mint, currants, and walnuts and stir to mix them. Sprinkle the dill on top, if using. Now you're ready to eat like an Iranian!

6. You can also refrigerate mast-o-khiyar overnight before serving. Letting the mixture sit will improve the dish's flavor.

•❖ Fresh fruit is a popular snack in Iran.

Dessert in Iran starts with fresh fruit, usually oranges, apples, pomegranates, or dates. Then tea and pastries are served. Popular pastries include *noghl* (slivers of almonds rolled in a sweet syrup) and *nokhodchi* (a cookie made from chickpea flour). Ice cream is a favorite dessert during Iran's hot summers.

Whether you're munching a sweet pastry or speeding down a snowy ski slope, Iran will charm and thrill you. Shaped by its complicated history and the religious beliefs of its people, Iran is a distinctive place. From its rugged mountains to its busy capital city, the country offers a wide range of experiences. Which part of Iran do you want to explore first?

GLOSSARY

ayatollah (eye-uh-TOE-luh) a title for a religious leader in Shia Islam

blasphemy (BLAS-fuh-me) an act that insults God or shows a lack of religious reverence

corruption (kuh-RUP-shuhn) a lack of integrity or ethical conduct

denominations (di-nah-muh-NAY-shuhnz) organized groups within a religion

dynasty (DYE-nuh-stee) a series of rulers who belong to the same family

embassy (EM-buh-see) the official office and home in a foreign country of an ambassador (a representative from a different country's government)

ethnic (ETH-nik) having to do with a group of people sharing the same national origins, language, or culture

evaporates (i-VAP-uh-rates) changes from a liquid to a gas

fast (FAST) going without eating food or without certain types of food during a set period

landlocked (LAND-lokt) surrounded on all sides by land

martyrs (MAHR-turz) people who are killed or made to suffer for their beliefs or for a specific cause

mosques (MAHSKS) Muslim places of worship

suburbs (SUB-urbz) areas with homes and businesses close to large cities

FOR MORE INFORMATION

Books

Habeeb, William Mark. *Iran*. Broomall, PA: Mason Crest, 2010.

Milivojevic, JoAnn. *Iran*. New York: Children's Press, 2008.

Ramen, Fred. *A Historical Atlas of Iran*. New York: Rosen, 2003.

Web Sites

Central Intelligence Agency: The World Factbook—Iran
https://www.cia.gov/library/publications/the-world-factbook/geos/ir.html
Find up-to-date information about Iran's government, people, geography, and economy.

Library of Congress: A Country Study—Iran
lcweb2.loc.gov/frd/cs/irtoc.html
Get in-depth information on Iran's history and society.

National Geographic Kids: Iran
kids.nationalgeographic.com/kids/places/find/iran
Check out photos, videos, maps, and other cool stuff related to Iran.

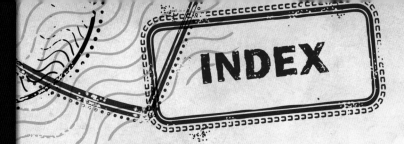

INDEX

ABOUT THE AUTHOR
G. S. Prentzas has written more than two dozen books for young readers. He has explored every continent except Antarctica. He hopes to visit Iran someday.